BOLD KIDS

**EDUCATIONAL FACTS
CHILDREN'S SCIENCE BOOK**

No part of this book may be reproduced or used in any way or form or by any means whether electronic or mechanical, this means that you cannot record or photocopy any material ideas or tips that are provided in this book.
Copyright 2022

All images in this book have been reproduced with the knowledge and prior consent of the artists concerned, and no responsibility is accepted by producer, publisher, or printer for any infringement of copyright or otherwise, arising from the contents of this publication.

FOOD CHAINS

There are many different types of food chains. The first chain starts with the green plant. This plant will become the source of nutrients for other animals in the chain. These animals will in turn consume plant products.

In the food chain, plants may be consumed by animals like rabbits, frogs, owls, and birds. Then, these animals will in turn eat other organisms. The cycle of energy and food continues to this day, and the whole cycle is known as a food chain.

The food chain shows the succession of energy and matter from the sun to living organisms. This is called a trophic ladder, with the first level being plants. Then, the next level is herbivores, followed by carnivores and tertiary consumers.

Ultimately, the food chain ends with the decomposers. In an ecosystem, every animal and plant species is dependent upon one another for its survival.

The energy transfer from one trophic level to the next decreases with the increase in trophic level. Only ten percent of energy from one trophic level is transferred to the next level. The rest is used up by metabolic processes.

A food chain typically has at least five levels. The food chain can be disrupted with devastating results. However, if you follow the food chain up, you will be able to get more energy in one pound of food. For example, a salad has more energy per pound than lettuce. It may not work for all species.

TROPHIC LEVELS

In nature, organisms are classified according to their trophic level, or feeding position. The first level of the food chain is occupied by producers, such as plants and trees, and it is followed by primary producers and herbivores.

The next two levels of the food chain are occupied by secondary consumers, such as animals that feed on these producers. The final trophic level is occupied by predators. There are many organisms that feed at more than one trophic level, such as omnivores and apex predators.

The first level of the food chain is the producer, which produces carbon dioxide and sugars through photosynthesis. These organisms include algae and plants. Their metabolic processes use carbon dioxide and light energy to produce glucose and other organic compounds, which then make their way up the food chain.

The food chain would be incomplete without the producer. This first level would then move up to the next trophic level. In the example of the food chain, the producer is a plant, which transforms carbon dioxide into glucose and oxygen.

After the primary producers, there are secondary consumers and apex consumers. Secondary consumers include all animals that eat herbivores, such as fish and birds. Apex consumers are larger organisms, such as apex predators.

Most marine animals are secondary consumers. This means that most fish, jellyfish, and crustaceans are the second and third-level consumers, respectively. But these species do not necessarily eat other organisms at the same level.

PHOTOSYNTHESIS

The process of photosynthesis provides carbon for organic molecules. Plants store this energy in their biological molecules, and the process also creates the oxygen needed by aerobic organisms like humans.

Moreover, photosynthesis helps the earth by removing CO_2 from the atmosphere. The interactive below helps students visualize this process and its roles in food chains. Photosynthesis is controlled by many factors, and students should check out maps of different ecosystems to better understand its role.

Photosynthetic plants are the most common autotrophs in terrestrial ecosystems. Photosynthesis occurs in all green plant tissues, but the majority of it occurs in leaves. Mesophyll cells are the primary sites of photosynthesis.

To facilitate the process, the leaves are equipped with stomata, which are tiny pores on the surface of the leaf. These pores allow carbon dioxide to enter the mesophyll and oxygen to leave.

All life on earth needs energy to live. Photosynthesis is essential for this process. Photosynthetic organisms help to store energy for future use. In addition to transferring carbon, the energy stored in food is also a source of food for other organisms.

This energy flows as a cycle on Earth. LLPA's photosynthesis lab offers an opportunity for students to explore this process firsthand. All life begins with light, so students will learn more about how photosynthesis works in food chains.

The plant is called a producer because it generates the majority of the food energy on Earth. Plants use some of this energy to perform their functions, while storing the rest. Plants can produce glucose or starch for consumption by other organisms.

These two types of foods are vital for the survival of humans, animals, and other animals. They also help clean the environment. However, they don't make any food themselves. Instead, they feed on other animals.

Ingram Content Group UK Ltd.
Milton Keynes UK
UKHW020820160623
423421UK00008B/35